ISBN 1-58660-464-3

Published by Barbour Books, an imprint of Barbour Publishing, Inc., P.O. Box 719, Uhrichsville, Ohio 44683, www.barbourbooks.com

 Member of the
Evangelical Christian
Publishers Association

Printed in China.
5 4 3 2 1

YOU ARE
A BLESSING

ELLYN SANNA

"The Lord has blessed me
because of you."

GENESIS 30:27

You have been a blessing in my life...

because you believe.

because you share.

because you love.

because I can always count on you.

YOU ARE A BLESSING

From the fullness of his grace
we have all received
one blessing after another.

Because You Believe

# YOU ARE A BLESSING

You have been a blessing in my life.
I learn just from watching you.
You see the clouds and know the sunshine is just beyond them.
You smell the rain and know the flowers will not wilt.
You hear the wind blow
and know the pollen will be spread from flower to flower.
Where I would see foreboding and disaster,
you see grace.
You have taught me to see, hear, and believe in new ways.
What a blessing you are to me.

You have told me many times:
"When happiness comes your way,
smile and say thank you.
It is gift to be enjoyed and savored.
It is a sign of God's presence."
Thank you for being
a sign of God's presence to me.
Thank you for sharing your faith.

We have only to believe.
And the more threatening. . .reality appears,
the more firmly and desperately must we believe.
Then, little by little,
we shall see the universal horror unbend,
and then smile upon us,
and then take us in its more human arms.

Pierre Teilhard de Chardin

When my world seems full of monsters,
thank you for your firm belief in God.
By the light of your faith,
I see God's smile hidden in even my most difficult days.

Gandhi said, "Be the change you want to see in the world."
Why not, "Be the blessing you would like others to be?"
You are that blessing to me.
Your faith in God inspires me,
and your life has left a mark on my heart.

May your life be like a snowflake,
which leaves a mark but not a stain.

AUTHOR UNKNOWN

Your life has shown me that
you and I are what is sacred in this world.
God comes to the world through us;
the holy is in the ordinary and the simple.
Knowing this, seeing this, is a blessing in itself.
Now I need to live what you have taught me.

Because You Share

YOU ARE A BLESSING

A candle loses nothing by lighting another candle;
its glow only gains a greater brilliance.
I watch you share the light of God with others,
and I see God's light add brilliance to their daily lives.
The light of your quiet faith is not diminished
through the sharing.
God's light is a special blessing shared by you.

*But the path of the just is as the shining light,
that shineth more and more unto the perfect day.*

PROVERBS 4:18 KJV

Human beings ought to. . .share
all the gifts they have received from God.

MEISTER ECKHART

Thank you for sharing with me
the gifts God gave you.
Your richness has enriched my life.

The Holy Nudge

God nudged us to rekindle our friendship.
He nudged me to ask you out to lunch.
As we ate, He nudged you to share the pain of years gone by.
He knew just what I needed to hear.
He knew that same pain was now mine.
He knew I needed to see an example of courage
and words of encouragement.
You gave me both.

I will hold you close in my heart.
I will remember your courage.
I will recall your encouragement.
I can truly say you are a blessing.
I offer a prayer of thanksgiving to God
for you, dear one, and
for the holy nudge He gave us both.
Thank you for sharing your heart with me.

You Are a Blessing

There is no such thing as "my bread."
All bread is ours and is given to me,
to others through me and to me through others.

MEISTER ECKHART

*The core of the Christian gospel is
a promise and an invitation to. . .
be at home in. . .
sharing the outgoing life of a non-excluding God
with the whole of creation.*

ELIZABETH TEMPLETON

The joy of receiving is far more than the gifts—
that when we receive graciously and gladly,
we reciprocate the gift with joy and gratitude;
and in that moment of shared happiness and understanding,
giver and receiver "connect."

JENNY WALTON

Thank you for sharing so much with me. . .
your time, your talents, your patience,
your resources, your faith, and your love.
Your life has blessed me.
You have helped me to see more clearly
a God who longs to share Himself with me.
Following your example
(and Christ's!),
I can no longer hoard my time and resources.
Everything is to be shared.

YOU ARE A BLESSING

You have taught me how to be a blessing.
You offer thanks for life's simple things.
You send a note or card
. . .to someone in pain,
. . .for a job well done,
. . .for a quiet kindness,
. . .celebrating a life experience,
like birth, graduation, or a new home.

You Are a Blessing

You speak words of encouragement to those who
. . .are in despair,
. . .are feeling pain,
. . .know loss,
. . .are discouraged.
You open your heart to listen,
and you whisper prayers in silence.
You have been a blessing through your acts of kindness.
You have taught me well. I will do the same. . .
passing on the blessing you have been to me.

*If you want your neighbor to see
what God's spirit will do for him,
let him see what it has done for you.*

Henry Ward Beecher

God has given us two hands—
One to receive with
And the other to give with.

BILLY GRAHAM

The more we receive in silent prayer,
the more we can give in active life.

MALCOLM MUGGERIDGE

Thank you for sharing
what God has given you!

Because You Love

If you affirm goodness, goodness will be there;
If you affirm love, love will be there;
If you affirm thankfulness, blessings will come.
A good place to begin is by giving praise and thanks to
Almighty God.

NORMAN VINCENT PEALE

*No act of kindness,
no matter how small, is ever wasted.*

AESOP

The only thing that counts
is faith expressing itself through love.

GALATIANS 5:6

He will cover you with his feathers,
And under his wings you will find refuge.

PSALM 91:4

There have been days when your voice on the phone,
your smile at my door,
your gentle hand on my shoulder
has felt to me
like God's feathers,
offering refuge.
Thank you.

Circle of Blessing

A circle has no beginning
and no ending.
The circle of blessing can begin at any point within it.
The circle is made up of
quiet actions, love,
simple gratitude,
forgiveness,
generous gifts,
trust,
precious memories,
a heart that knows what to remember
and what to forget.

God's love and presence holds the circle secure.
Thank you for your part in this circle of blessing.
As you encounter others along
the faith journey of your life,
you use this circle to bring
beauty into the lives of others.
Your love adds new loveliness to God's world.

Empathy is your pain in my heart.

JESS LAIR

A loving heart is the truest wisdom.

CHARLES DICKENS

Thank you for loving me enough to share my pain.
Thank you for the wisdom of your love.
Thank you for blessing me.

Words have the power to give life or to take life. . .
to create life or to destroy life.
Words live a long time in memory.
So often, I see you give life with a simple blessing. . .
a few kind words, words of encouragement,
words of sympathy, words filled with joy,
words of gratitude, words of love.
Your words create life.

He alone loves the Creator perfectly
who manifests a pure love for his neighbor.

VENERABLE BEDE

The first duty of love is to listen.

PAUL TILLICH

Thank you for all the times you simply
sat beside me and listened.
Thank you for loving God through me.
Thank you for showing me God's love in you.

*Because I Can
Always Count on You*

One can rely on a friend.
As a friend one is a person
for other people to rely on.
A friend remains a friend,
even in disaster, even in guilt.

JURGEN MOLTMANN

Thank you for always being there.
When I'm right. . .
and when I'm wrong,
you always stick by me.
What a blessing you are to me!

Grace Notes

I don't know anything about music, but recently I learned that in music a "grace note" is an extra embellishment that gives the lift to a song. In life grace is the unearned, unexpected, undeserved, unconditional note that turns our sighs into songs. We can all offer that grace in our relationships.

We can listen—even when what we are hearing is boring. By listening we offer grace.

We can be slow to react to another, not judging too quickly because the other may be acting out of his or her own pain, and our refusal to react in anger will offer grace.

We can forgive, even when we are hurt and forgiveness is not asked. That will be a marvelous act of grace.

Without the grace notes singing in our souls, the walk through the valley of the shadow is a bleak journey to the sound of a bass drum. But with the grace note, every now and then our walk breaks out into a dance.

Unknown

You have added grace notes to my life. . .
and even caused me to dance.

Our duty is not to see through one another
but to see one another through.

LEONARD SWEET

*A true friend is one who is there for you
when he would rather be anywhere else.*

LEN WEIN

You should rely on love.

HADEWIJCH OF BRABANT

Whenever I've needed someone to share my joy,
or someone to hold me when my world rips to pieces,
you're there. And I know you will be—tomorrow, always.

MAYA V. PATEL

YOU ARE A BLESSING

When I called upon God to show Himself to me,
He has blessed me with. . .
a letter bearing good news,
a caring voice on the phone,
a forgiving heart,
an invitation to share a cup of tea,
a ride to church,
a knock at the door,
a new beginning.
God showed Himself through friends, both old and new.
I am blessed once more!

*Great opportunities
to help others seldom come,
but small ones surround us daily.*

SALLY KOCH

Thank you
for taking advantage of all those small opportunities
to be a blessing in my life!

You Are a Blessing

Friendship, like the immortality of the soul,
is too good to be believed.
When friendships are real,
they are not glass threads or frost work,
but the solidest things we know.

RALPH WALDO EMERSON

Your presence in my life
is like solid ground that never shakes beneath my feet.
I know I can rely on you,
and I am grateful.

Love. . .puts up with anything,
Trusts God always,
Always looks for the best,
Never looks back,
But keeps going to the end.
Love never dies.

1 CORINTHIANS 13:4, 7–8 THE MESSAGE

Thank you for putting up with me.
Thank you for always being there.
How your love has blessed my life!

Another word for blessing. . .
YOU!

May the grace of Christ our Savior,
And the Father's boundless love,
With the Holy Spirit's favor,
Rest upon you from above.

JOHN NEWTON